THE JPS B'NAI MITZVAH TORAH COMMENTARY

Be-shallaḥ (Exodus 13:17–17:16)
Haftarah (Judges 4:4–5:31)

Rabbi Jeffrey K. Salkin

The Jewish Publication Society · Philadelphia
University of Nebraska Press · Lincoln

INTRODUCTION

News flash: the most important thing about becoming bar or bat mitzvah isn't the party. Nor is it the presents. Nor even being able to celebrate with your family and friends—as wonderful as those things are. Nor is it even standing before the congregation and reading the prayers of the liturgy—as important as that is.

No, the most important thing about becoming bar or bat mitzvah is sharing Torah with the congregation. And why is that? Because of all Jewish skills, that is the most important one.

Here is what is true about rites of passage: you can tell what a culture values by the tasks it asks its young people to perform on their way to maturity. In American culture, you become responsible for driving, responsible for voting, and yes, responsible for drinking responsibly.

In some cultures, the rite of passage toward maturity includes some kind of trial, or a test of strength. Sometimes, it is a kind of "outward bound" camping adventure. Among the Maasai tribe in Africa, it is traditional for a young person to hunt and kill a lion. In some Hispanic cultures, fifteen year-old girls celebrate the *quinceañera*, which marks their entrance into maturity.

What is Judaism's way of marking maturity? It combines both of these rites of passage: *responsibility* and *test*. You show that you are on your way to becoming a *responsible* Jewish adult through a public *test* of strength and knowledge—reading or chanting Torah, and then teaching it to the congregation.

This is the most important Jewish ritual mitzvah (commandment), and that is how you demonstrate that you are, truly, bar or bat mitzvah—old enough to be responsible for the mitzvot.

What Is Torah?

So, what exactly is the Torah? You probably know this already, but let's review.

The Torah (teaching) consists of "the five books of Moses," sometimes also called the *chumash* (from the Hebrew word *chameish,* which means "five"), or, sometimes, the Greek word Pentateuch (which means "the five teachings").

Here are the five books of the Torah, with their common names and their Hebrew names.

> Genesis (The beginning), which in Hebrew is Bere'shit (from the first words—"When God began to create"). Bere'shit spans the years from Creation to Joseph's death in Egypt. Many of the Bible's best stories are in Genesis: the creation story itself; Adam and Eve in the Garden of Eden; Cain and Abel; Noah and the Flood; and the tales of the Patriarchs and Matriarchs, Abraham, Isaac, Jacob, Sarah, Rebekah, Rachel, and Leah. It also includes one of the greatest pieces of world literature, the story of Joseph, which is actually the oldest complete novel in history, comprising more than one-quarter of all Genesis.

> Exodus (Getting out), which in Hebrew is Shemot (These are the names). Exodus begins with the story of the Israelite slavery in Egypt. It then moves to the rise of Moses as a leader, and the Israelites' liberation from slavery. After the Israelites leave Egypt, they experience the miracle of the parting of the Sea of Reeds (or "Red Sea"); the giving of the Ten Commandments at Mount Sinai; the idolatry of the Golden Calf; and the design and construction of the Tabernacle and of the ark for the original tablets of the law, which our ancestors carried with them in the desert. Exodus also includes various ethical and civil laws, such as "You shall not wrong a stranger or oppress him, for you were strangers in the land of Egypt" (22:20).

> Leviticus (about the Levites), or, in Hebrew, Va-yikra' (And God called). It goes into great detail about the kinds of sacrifices that the ancient Israelites brought as offerings; the laws of ritual purity; the animals that were permitted and forbidden for eating (the beginnings of the tradition of kashrut, the Jewish dietary laws); the diagnosis of various skin diseases; the ethical laws of holiness; the ritual calendar of the Jewish year; and various agricultural laws concerning the treatment of the Land of Israel. Leviticus is basically the manual of ancient Judaism.

➤ **Numbers (because the book begins with the census of the Israelites), or, in Hebrew, Be-midbar (In the wilderness).** The book describes the forty years of wandering in the wilderness and the various rebellions against Moses. The constant theme: "Egypt wasn't so bad. Maybe we should go back." The greatest rebellion against Moses was the negative reports of the spies about the Land of Israel, which discouraged the Israelites from wanting to move forward into the land. For that reason, the "wilderness generation" must die off before a new generation can come into maturity and finish the journey.

➤ **Deuteronomy (The repetition of the laws of the Torah), or, in Hebrew, Devarim (The words).** The final book of the Torah is, essentially, Moses's farewell address to the Israelites as they prepare to enter the Land of Israel. Here we find various laws that had been previously taught, though sometimes with different wording. Much of Deuteronomy contains laws that will be important to the Israelites as they enter the Land of Israel—laws concerning the establishment of a monarchy and the ethics of warfare. Perhaps the most famous passage from Deuteronomy contains the *Shema*, the declaration of God's unity and uniqueness, and the *Ve-ahavta*, which follows it. Deuteronomy ends with the death of Moses on Mount Nebo as he looks across the Jordan Valley into the land that he will not enter.

Jews read the Torah in sequence—starting with Bere'shit right after Simchat Torah in the autumn, and then finishing Devarim on the following Simchat Torah. Each Torah portion is called a parashah (division; sometimes called a *sidrah*, a place in the order of the Torah reading). The stories go around in a full circle, reminding us that we can always gain more insights and more wisdom from the Torah. This means that if you don't "get" the meaning this year, don't worry—it will come around again.

And What Else? The Haftarah

We read or chant the Torah from the Torah scroll—the most sacred thing that a Jewish community has in its possession. The Torah is written without vowels, and the ability to read it and chant it is part of the challenge and the test.

But there is more to the synagogue reading. Every Torah reading has an accompanying haftarah reading. Haftarah means "conclusion," because there was once a time when the service actually ended with that reading. Some scholars believe that the reading of the haftarah originated at a time when non-Jewish authorities outlawed the reading of the Torah, and the Jews read the haftarah sections instead. In fact, in some synagogues, young people who become bar or bat mitzvah read very little Torah and instead read the entire haftarah portion.

The haftarah portion comes from the Nevi'im, the prophetic books, which are the second part of the Jewish Bible. It is either read or chanted from a Hebrew Bible, or maybe from a booklet or a photocopy.

The ancient sages chose the haftarah passages because their themes reminded them of the words or stories in the Torah text. Sometimes, they chose *haftarah* with special themes in honor of a festival or an upcoming festival.

Not all books in the prophetic section of the Hebrew Bible consist of prophecy. Several are historical. For example:

The book of Joshua tells the story of the conquest and settlement of Israel.

The book of Judges speaks of the period of early tribal rulers who would rise to power, usually for the purpose of uniting the tribes in war against their enemies. Some of these leaders are famous: Deborah, the great prophetess and military leader, and Samson, the biblical strong man.

The books of Samuel start with Samuel, the last judge, and then move to the creation of the Israelite monarchy under Saul and David (approximately 1000 BCE).

The books of Kings tell of the death of King David, the rise of King Solomon, and how the Israelite kingdom split into the Northern Kingdom of Israel and the Southern Kingdom of Judah (approximately 900 BCE).

And then there are the books of the prophets, those spokesmen for God whose words fired the Jewish conscience. Their names are immortal: Isaiah, Jeremiah, Ezekiel, Amos, Hosea, among others.

Someone once said: "There is no evidence of a biblical prophet ever being invited back a second time for dinner." Why? Because the prophets were tough. They had no patience for injustice, apathy, or hypocrisy. No one escaped their criticisms. Here's what they taught:

> - God commands the Jews to behave decently toward one another. In fact, God cares more about basic ethics and decency than about ritual behavior.
> - God chose the Jews *not* for special privileges, but for special duties to humanity.
> - As bad as the Jews sometimes were, there was always the possibility that they would improve their behavior.
> - As bad as things might be now, it will not always be that way. Someday, there will be universal justice and peace. Human history is moving forward toward an ultimate conclusion that some call the Messianic Age: a time of universal peace and prosperity for the Jewish people and for all the people of the world.

Your Mission—To Teach Torah to the Congregation

On the day when you become bar or bat mitzvah, you will be reading, or chanting, Torah—in Hebrew. You will be reading, or chanting, the haftarah—in Hebrew. That is the major skill that publicly marks the becoming of bar or bat mitzvah. But, perhaps even more important than that, you need to be able to teach something about the Torah portion, and perhaps the haftarah as well.

And that is where this book comes in. It will be a very valuable resource for you, and your family, in the b'nai mitzvah process.

Here is what you will find in it:

> - A brief **summary** of every Torah portion. This is a basic overview of the portion; and, while it might not refer to everything in the Torah portion, it will explain its most important aspects.
> - A list of the **major ideas** in the Torah portion. The purpose: to make the Torah portion real, in ways that we can relate to. Every Torah portion contains unique ideas, and when you put all

of those ideas together, you actually come up with a list of Judaism's most important ideas.

> Two **divrei Torah** ("words of Torah," or "sermonettes") for each portion. These *divrei Torah* explain significant aspects of the Torah portion in accessible, reader-friendly language. Each *devar Torah* contains references to **traditional** Jewish sources (those that were written before the modern era), as well as **modern** sources and quotes. We have searched, far and wide, to find sources that are unusual, interesting, and not just the "same old stuff" that many people already know about the Torah portion. Why did we include these minisermons in the volume? Not because we want you to simply copy those sermons and pass them off as your own (that would be cheating), though you are free to quote from them. We included them so that you can see what is possible—how you can try to make meaning for yourself out of the words of Torah.

> **Connections:** This is perhaps the most valuable part. It's a list of questions that you can ask yourself, or that others might help you think about—any of which can lead to the creation of your *devar Torah*.

Note: you don't have to like everything that's in a particular Torah portion. Some aren't that loveable. Some are hard to understand; some are about religious practices that people today might find confusing, and even offensive; some contain ideas that we might find totally outmoded.

But this doesn't have to get in the way. After all, most kids spend a lot of time thinking about stories that contain ideas that modern people would find totally bizarre. Any good medieval fantasy story falls into that category.

And we also believe that, if you spend just a little bit of time with those texts, you can begin to understand what the author was trying to say.

This volume goes one step further. Sometimes, the haftarah comes off as a second thought, and no one really thinks about it. We have tried to solve that problem by including a **summary** of each haftarah, and then a mini-sermon on the haftarah. This will help you learn how these sacred words are relevant to today's world, and even to your own life.

All Bible quotations come from the NJPS translation, which is found in the many different editions of the JPS TANAKH; in the Conservative movement's *Etz Hayim: Torah and Commentary;* in the Reform movement's *Torah: A Modern Commentary;* and in other Bible commentaries and study guides.

How Do I Write a *Devar Torah?*

It really is easier than it looks.

There are many ways of thinking about the *devar Torah.* It is, of course, a short sermon on the meaning of the Torah (and, perhaps, the haftarah) portion. It might even be helpful to think of the *devar Torah* as a "book report" on the portion itself.

The most important thing you can know about this sacred task is: *Learn* the words. *Love* the words. Teach people what it could mean to *live* the words.

Here's a basic outline for a *devar Torah:*

"My Torah portion is (name of portion) _____,
   from the book of _____ , chapter
   _____.

"In my Torah portion, we learn that_____
   (Summary of portion)
"For me, the most important lesson of this Torah portion is (what
   is the best thing in the portion? Take the portion as a whole;
   your *devar Torah* does not have to be only, or specifically, on the
   verses that you are reading).
"As I learned my Torah portion, I found myself wondering:
   ➤ *Raise a question that the Torah portion itself raises.*
   ➤ *"Pick a fight"* with the portion. Argue with it.
   ➤ *Answer a question* that is listed in the "Connections" section of
     each Torah portion.
   ➤ *Suggest a question to your rabbi* that you would want the rabbi
     to answer in his or her own *devar Torah* or sermon.

"I have lived the values of the Torah by _____
(here, you can talk about how the Torah portion relates to your
own life. If you have done a mitzvah project, you can talk about
that here).

How To Keep It from Being Boring
(and You from Being Bored)

Some people just don't like giving traditional speeches. From our per-
spective, that's really okay. Perhaps you can teach Torah in a different
way—one that makes sense to you.

› Write an "open letter" to one of the characters in your Torah portion. "Dear Abraham: I hope that your trip to Canaan was not too
  hard . . ." "Dear Moses: Were you afraid when you got the Ten
  Commandments on Mount Sinai? I sure would have been . . ."
› Write a news story about what happens. Imagine yourself to
  be a television or news reporter. "Residents of neighboring cities were horrified yesterday as the wicked cities of Sodom and
  Gomorrah were burned to the ground. Some say that God was
  responsible . . ."
› Write an imaginary interview with a character in your Torah portion.
› Tell the story from the point of view of another character, or a mi-
  nor character, in the story. For instance, tell the story of the Gar-
  den of Eden from the point of view of the serpent. Or the story
  of the Binding of Isaac from the point of view of the ram, which
  was substituted for Isaac as a sacrifice. Or perhaps the story of
  the sale of Joseph from the point of view of his coat, which was
  stripped off him and dipped in a goat's blood.
› Write a poem about your Torah portion.
› Write a song about your Torah portion.
› Write a play about your Torah portion, and have some friends act
  it out with you.
› Create a piece of artwork about your Torah portion.

The bottom line is: Make this a joyful experience. Yes—it could
even be fun.

The Very Last Thing You Need to Know at This Point

The Torah scroll is written without vowels. Why? Don't *sofrim* (Torah scribes) know the vowels?

Of course they do.

So, why do they leave the vowels out?

One reason is that the Torah came into existence at a time when sages were still arguing about the proper vowels, and the proper pronunciation.

But here is another reason: The Torah text, as we have it today, and as it sits in the scroll, is actually *an unfinished work*. Think of it: the words are just sitting there. Because they have no vowels, it is as if they have no voice.

When we read the Torah publicly, we give voice to the ancient words. And when we find meaning in those ancient words, and we talk about those meanings, those words jump to life. They enter our lives. They make our world deeper and better.

Mazal tov to you, and your family. This is your journey toward Jewish maturity. Love it.

THE TORAH

❖ Be-shallaḥ: Exodus 13:17–17:16

You'd have thought that Pharaoh would have finally understood what was going on. The plagues that had devastated Egypt should have been enough of a lesson in how not to mess with God or the Israelites. But, no. As the Israelites finally escape Egypt, Pharaoh changes his mind and he sends his armies to pursue them.

Coming to the Sea of Reeds (sometimes called the Red Sea), the Israelites are faced with almost certain death, until God splits the sea for them and they walk through the parted waters. The sea closes back on the Egyptian armies and they drown.

This miracle prompts the Israelites to sing the "Song at the Sea" (which is why the Shabbat associated with this Torah reading is also called Shabbat Shirah, the "Shabbat of song"). But this miracle doesn't succeed in making the Israelites happy; soon, they are complaining about the lack of food and water. To make matters worse, the Amalekites attack the Israelites in the desert—a battle that the Israelites actually win.

Summary

- ‣ There are no shortcuts through the wilderness! God takes the Israelites the long way. Moses carries the bones of Joseph with him, remembering that Joseph's brothers had promised to bury him in the Land of Israel. (13:17–19)
- ‣ Pharaoh and his armies pursue the Israelites, and they come to the Sea of Reeds (sometimes also referred to as "the Red Sea"). The sea parts, the Israelites march through the parted waters, the waters come back together again to drown the Egyptian soldiers, and the Israelites sing. Moses's sister, Miriam, leads the women in joyous song. (14:10–15:21)
- ‣ There is a shortage of food, and the people complain. (16:1–11)
- ‣ God rains manna—a white, flaky substance—on the Israelites. They gather the manna, with a double portion for Shabbat. (16:13–36)
- ‣ There is a shortage of water, and the people keep complaining. God tells Moses to hit a rock so that it will produce water. It works! (17:1–7)
- ‣ Amalek attacks the Israelites. They fight the Amalekites, and the Israelites defeat them. (17:8–16)

The Big Ideas

> **The road to freedom is rarely short and easy.** It always seems to have twists and turns and even U-turns. This is true not only for the Jews, but also for other groups that have fought for freedom.

> **In our personal journeys we always travel with pieces of our past.** That is why the Israelites took the bones of Joseph with them. They knew that his final resting place could not be Egypt, but rather the Land of Israel.

> **The parting of the sea was the miracle that "created" the Jewish people.** True—there are scientific explanations for what happened at the sea; perhaps it was a tidal wave or some other natural occurrence. But its parting is a symbol; it mirrors the moment of creation, when God separates the upper waters from the lower waters. At the moment that God parts the waters, the Jewish people is created.

> **Women have their own voices in Judaism.** Those voices have always been important and cherished, even when it has seemed that they are barely audible. That is the lesson of Miriam's involvement in the Song at the Sea.

> **Jews love to complain!** That is true throughout Jewish history and even and especially in Jewish humor. It starts right here. Complaining is a constant theme in the story of the Exodus and the wandering in the wilderness.

Divrei Torah

WHY NOT THE EASY WAY?

Time for an old Jewish joke. "Why did it take the Israelites forty years to go through the wilderness and get to the Land of Israel? Because Moses refused to stop and ask for directions!"

That's sort of how the Torah portion begins. It tells us that God did not lead the people by way of the land of the Philistines, "although it was nearer." Imagine that—if the Israelites had traveled across the land of the Philistines (or, to be more precise, the land that the ancient Philistines would someday occupy), across the top of the Sinai Peninsula, they would have gotten to the Land of Israel in almost no time at all.

So, why didn't God take the Israelites the easy, short way? The text says that the people would have been afraid "when they see war," which probably means that those borders were heavily fortified. Or perhaps it was precisely *because* it was the easy way. That's how Rashi, the great medieval commentator, understood it: "It was easy to return by that road to Egypt." God wanted to teach the Israelites the importance of perseverance. God was afraid that they might return; if they had an easy time of it, it would be more tempting to turn back if things got rough.

When we travel, we usually like going the shortest way; that's why we have a GPS. But that's not the way it is in real life. There's a modern expression that we sometimes use: "No pain, no gain." It is true of athletes, great artists and musicians, and anyone who has had to work for something. If the task is too easy, then we won't value it.

Rabbi Steven Moskowitz writes: "Too often we want the shortcut. Too many students for example read *Spark Notes* rather than reading *Hamlet*. The long, hard work, the struggle, is the greatest lesson and provides the most lasting meaning. You can only appreciate Shakespeare and what he teaches us about life if you read Shakespeare."

What is true about appreciating great literature is certainly true of national liberation movements. Those movements never have it easy. Think of the struggles that the Reverend Martin Luther King Jr. had to endure (and it's a sweet coincidence that this Torah portion often comes right around his birthday). The title of Nelson Mandela's autobiography is *No Easy Walk to Freedom*. It was true of the struggle of

Soviet Jews to gain their freedom. And it was definitely true of the story of Israel and Zionism.

And it is almost definitely true of kids who are preparing to become bar and bat mitzvah! It's not easy. It's not meant to be. It probably shouldn't be. Because if it were, how much would we value it?

One last thing: the long way through the wilderness includes stopping at Mount Sinai, where the Israelites will receive the Ten Commandments. The long way includes the encounter with God.

GET READY TO JUMP!

Whenever you think of the meaning of faith, consider this: every time you jump into a swimming pool, you have faith that since the last time you jumped into the pool the laws of physics have not changed. Every time you board an airplane the same thing happens. You have faith that the pilot knows how to fly the plane and that planes can still fly through the air.

But those examples are about things that have already happened in the past. What about those things that you have never encountered yet? Would you have the same kind of faith?

That was precisely what happened when the Israelites got to the shores of the Sea of Reeds. The Egyptians were behind them, the sea was in front of them. Either way they turned, there was the probability of death, either by the sword or by drowning. What should they do?

Here is where the richness of the Jewish tradition comes alive. What happened at the edge of the water? Some ancient sages said that each tribe demanded the privilege of going in first. Others said quite the opposite: each tribe demanded that the others go in first. Like we've already learned, in this Torah portion it would seem that the Israelites discovered the fine art of complaining—and, some say, that is what they all did at the shores of the sea.

Except for one man. As a midrash says, "When Israel stood by the sea, the tribes stood arguing with each other, one saying, 'I will go in first,' and the other saying, 'I will go in first.' At that moment, Nahshon ben Amminadab of the tribe of Judah jumped into the waves of the sea and waded in." And at that moment, the waters parted and the people were able to walk through to safety and freedom.

This is what we sometimes call "a leap of faith." Nahshon chose not to be afraid. Because he jumped, the tradition says that he would be the ancestor of King David, and he would have the honor of being the first person to bring an offering at the dedication of the Tabernacle.

Rabbi Sid Schwarz teaches: "Maybe you don't believe that the miracle happened as the midrash suggests it did. But you don't have to. Every great moment in history, every person who achieves greatness, every person who conquers the fears that may have paralyzed them for years has that Nachshon moment."

Even in an age in which God splits seas, the Torah places tremendous emphasis on human beings taking the first step. God will not save the Israelites unless and until they are willing to go forward into the unknown. The sea will not split until someone is ready to proceed. It is only once the Israelites act, boldly and dauntlessly, that God's miraculous intervention sets in.

Connections

> What do you think happened at the sea? Was it a miracle, or a natural occurrence? What have been some "miracles" in your life? What were they like?

> When have you imitated Nahshon? When have you jumped right into something? What were your feelings before you did it? What were your feelings afterward?

> Who are the men or women in your (extended) family who have taken a risk in their lives or in their careers? What did they do and why?

> Who are some people in history who have imitated Nahshon?

> What are some examples of things that have taken time and effort in your life?

THE HAFTARAH

❖ Be-shallaḥ: Judges 4:4–5:31

If you ever cruise through radio stations, you might discover that some are devoted totally to oldies, classic rock songs, usually from the 1970s and earlier. This week's Torah portion contains one of the oldest songs in human history—*Shirat ha-Yam*, the song at the Sea of Reeds (or Red Sea) that Moses, Miriam, and the Israelites sang after the waters of the sea parted and they were able to cross victoriously. It is read on Shabbat Shirah, the Shabbat of Song. The poem, scholars tell us, is a very old form of Hebrew, and may have been written within a few generations of the Exodus.

The song, or poem that appears in this haftarah is likely as old as the one in Exodus, if not older. It is the song of Deborah. This poem is also in archaic Hebrew, and may have been written immediately after the events described, or soon thereafter.

The story of Deborah takes place during the era in Israel's early history known as the period of the judges, and the stories of that time are found in the biblical book of Judges. The judges were actually tribal chieftains and military leaders who welded the tribes of Israel into loose and temporary confederations, largely for the purpose of fighting the Philistines. Deborah was not only a chieftain and a warrior; she was also a prophetess, just like Miriam in this week's corresponding Torah portion. She counsels the Israelite general Barak to draw the Canaanite general Sisera into battle, and, due to Deborah's help, Barak is victorious. The song of Deborah commemorates that victory.

Women Power

There have been many famous lines by American politicians, and here's one of them. In a presidential debate, someone asked a candidate why he had not hired more women for top positions. He responded that if he were president he would turn to the "binders full of women" for candidates to fill cabinet positions.

This week, both the Torah and the haftarah are like binders full of women. In the Torah portion, we have Miriam leading the women of Israel in song at the crossing of the Sea of Reeds (or Red Sea). And, in the haftarah, you have Deborah, the military leader.

The late Jewish singer-composer Debbie Friedman, who notably sang about Miriam, also sang a great song about Deborah: "Devorah the prophet, a woman of fire, her torch in hand. She led the Israelites to victory. Barak said, 'Devorah, I cannot fight, unless you are standing right by my side!'" Friedman based her own song on Deborah's, which states, "But Barak said to her, 'If you will go with me, I will go; if not, I will not go.' 'Very well, I will go with you,' she answered. 'However, there will be no glory for you in the course you are taking, for then the Lord will deliver Sisera into the hands of a woman" (4:8–9).

There are two more women you need to meet.

The first is Jael, the wife of Heber the Kenite (4:17–21). She happens not to be an Israelite, but she is sympathetic to them. She is one tough lady. Sisera, the Canaanite general, flees to her tent, and Jael invites him to enter. She feeds him, which makes him sleepy, and, as he begins to snooze, Jael assassinates him. And, because of this, Israel is victorious over the Canaanite army. The song of Deborah praises her actions.

And there is one more woman whom the song of Deborah mentions. She shows up at the end, and it is easy to miss her. But don't. She is very important.

But first, let's think about the sound of the shofar (the ram's horn) on the High Holy Days. Have you ever noticed that it sounds like a cry? It is written in the Talmud, "One authority thought that this means that it sounds like a long sigh, and the other that it sounds like short, piercing cries."

Whose cries? A woman's. Fine, but which woman? The Talmud says: the mother of Sisera.

Let's recall the scene. Sisera's mother is waiting for him to come home. "Where is that boy? He must be out pillaging." A few hours later: "He must have stopped off with the others to get a drink." A few hours later: "Where could he be? Why hasn't he called?"

As the poem relates,

Through the window peered Sisera's mother,
Behind the lattice she whined:
"Why is his chariot so long in coming?
Why so late the clatter of his wheels?"
The wisest of her ladies give answer;
She, too, replies to herself:
"They must be dividing the spoil they have found:
A damsel or two for each man,
Spoil of dyed cloths for Sisera,
Spoil of embroidered cloths,
A couple of embroidered cloths
Round every neck as spoil.
    (5:28–30)

But Sisera is not coming home. When his mother discovers that her son is dead, she wails—and the ancient Rabbis connect her wails to the origins of the shofar blasts.

Why should we care about this mother of a barbaric Canaanite general? Because, even though she is "the enemy," we can empathize with her. Her son has died. The ability to empathize, even with our enemies, is a major Jewish character trait.

❖ Notes

CPSIA information can be obtained
at www.ICGtesting.com
Printed in the USA
LVHW08s0951050818
585984LV00004B/423/P